Read To Me Bedtime Stories Presents:

The Adventures of Hammy the Hamster

By Jamal Q'ettelle

First edition 2024

Dedication

This book is dedicated to my beautiful daughter Sapphire and her pet Hamster Hammy.

Acknowledgement

I am truly grateful for the opportunity to write these books, and I thank God for guiding me along this journey. I want to extend my heartfelt appreciation to my beautiful wife, Chantal, whose unwavering support and inspiration have been my driving force.

I would also like to thank my editor, Sherell Bernard for her patience and guidance in making this book a reality.

Special thanks to Jerrard, Melissa, and Javier Thorpe, Whitney and Atarah Collins, T'Shura La Fond, Maryam Greenridge and Xavi Thomas. I am also immensely thankful to everyone who has taken the time to read samples of my book and offer words of encouragement.

Your encouragement and support mean the world to me, fuelling my passion to continue this series. With every word I write, I aim to bring smiles to children's faces and spread joy through storytelling.

Thank you, and may God continue to bless us all abundantly.

Jamal

Table Of Contents

Part One: Through the Eyes of Sapphire

Hello, fellow book bugs! The story begins as we look through the eyes of a little girl named Sapphire; she is kind, fun and loving. However, because she is an only child, she is sometimes lonely. She leads us on an adventurous journey as she discovers her love for animals. Through this little journey, she will encounter excitement, happiness, and sorrow. How will it end? As we look through part one, sit back and share in this epic adventure and see what happens.

Chapter One: The Chosen Pet

Once upon a time in the village of Riverside, lived a little girl named Sapphire. Sapphire lived with her mom and dad. She was very kindhearted and loving. She always did her chores, always did her homework, and loved animals. One of her favorite things to do was visit the zoo with her mom and dad. She loved seeing the animals there. Her favorite animal to look at was the giraffe. They were so tall, and she was amazed at how they could reach the high branches of trees to eat. After visits to the zoo, she enjoyed going on picnics at the Savannah next to the zoo and playing games with her dad.

However, Sapphire was an only child. She had no friends living close by as there weren't any kids her age around. It sometimes made her feel lonely. One day, she went to her cousin Zariah's birthday party and saw one of the gifts she received was a rabbit. Zariah named the rabbit Benny. Benny was big and white and loved to hop around. Sapphire fell in love with Benny. She soon wanted a pet of her own. Suddenly she had an idea— she could ask her parents for a pet!

The next day she approached her dad. He was sitting on the couch watching a football match. "Hi Dad, can I have a pet please?" asked

Sapphire as she lightly tapped his shoulder. "What kind of pet would you like to have?" her father asked, squinting his eyes as he looked at her. "Um… I don't know," said Sapphire, "Maybe a rabbit like my cousin Zariah, a cat, or even a giraffe like the ones in the zoo."

Her father then laughed, "We definitely cannot get you a giraffe, it's way too big."

"Well, what about a rabbit or a cat?"

"Hmm, well you know taking care of a pet requires a lot of responsibility, especially for a 6-year-old girl. Do you think you are ready for that?"

"Yes Daddy," she said, smiling with excitement and confidence.

"Tell you what." Her father placed his hand on her shoulder. "If you do well in your test at the end of the year, your mommy and I will take you to the pet store and let you pick out whichever pet you would like."

"You have a deal, Daddy!" Sapphire's face was beaming with joy. She was really happy because she knew if she studied hard, she would get a pet of her choice. So Sapphire studied every day and, when her test was finished, she collected her report card and saw that she got an A+.

Sapphire was very happy because she knew her parents would be taking her to the pet store to get her new pet. She couldn't wait to see them later that day. When school was over, Sapphire's grandmother came to pick her up. Sapphire was so excited to tell her grandmother how well she did in her end of term test.

"Granny, Granny I got an A+ in my test." She handed her grandmother her report card, her face beaming.

"That's very good dear," her grandmother said as she read the report card, "Let's go for ice cream."

Sapphire was excited when they got to the ice cream shop. She told her grandmother she wanted a chocolate chip ice cream with a wafer bowl. Sapphire got two scoops of chocolate chip ice cream and her grandmother got a coconut ice cream in a cup.

While they were sitting eating their ice cream, Sapphire's grandmother turned to Sapphire and asked, "What would you like your parents to get you for doing so well in school? Will you want them to get you the new Barbie doll?"

"Nope," Sapphire replied, shaking her head.

"Oh, then it has to be that Pony set you always talked about," Grandma said, wiping smudges of ice cream on Sapphire's chin and around her mouth with a napkin.

"No, it's not." Sapphire giggled.

"Hmm, well tell me what is this mystery present you would like to get, dear."

"I will be getting my very first pet," Sapphire replied happily, stretching her arms in the air.

Later that evening, Sapphire's grandmother dropped her off at home and left. Sapphire raced inside as quickly as she could. When she got to the living room, she saw her dad was reading a book, and she could hear the sounds of her mom preparing dinner in the kitchen. She quickly threw off her book bag and started looking for her report card.

"Is everything okay honey?" her mother said as she came out of the kitchen and began setting plates on the dinner table. Sapphire took out her report card and showed it to her parents reminding them of their promise. Her parents were very proud. Her dad gave her a big hug and her mom kissed her on her cheek. They told her they would take her to the pet store on Saturday.

That night, Sapphire was so excited she was barely able to sleep. Saturday morning, she awoke at 5:00 a.m., ran over to her parents' bedroom, and jumped on the bed, waking them up. "Mom, Dad today's the day!" Sapphire said excitedly, jumping on the bed.

"Yes, it is," her dad agreed, covering his stomach as she jumped on him. "Please go back to bed Sapphire, the pet store does not open until 9:00 a.m."

"Okay Daddy," Sapphire ran back to her room. She started thinking about what pet she was going to choose. *Should I get a puppy? Or maybe a rabbit like Bennie or even a fish?* She wondered as she lay on her bed, looking up at the ceiling and smiling to herself.

Later that morning, Sapphire and her parents arrived at the pet store; there were a lot of different animals to see. In the bird section, she saw parrots, parakeets, and other birds she didn't know about. They were all so pretty, in different colors flying about their cages as Sapphire and her parents walked by.

She passed the reptile section and saw different types of snakes and lizards. She saw one of the workers at the pet store feeding rats to a small snake, which her dad told her was called a boa constrictor. This scared her, so she quickly walked past that section.

She then approached a brownish animal with a long tail eating almond nuts. She was familiar with almond nuts because she had an almond tree in her backyard.

"What kind of animal is that Daddy?" she asked, pointing her finger.

"Oh, that's a squirrel." Her father chuckled. Sapphire then noticed an aquarium with a castle in it and a black and brown turtle swam out from behind the castle. *That turtle is so pretty,* she thought, watching the turtle swim around the aquarium. Then she saw one of the most beautiful fishes she had ever seen. Swimming out of the castle in the aquarium, was a brightly colored fish; its colors sparkled as it swam around in the aquarium, and its long colorful tail drifted in the water.

"What type of fish is that one Daddy? ... It's beautiful!" Sapphire pointed at the fish, smiling. It had so many colors: blue, green, orange, purple with black and white spots.

"That's an Angel Fish," replied her father, "it's a tropical fish and one of the most beautiful fishes you can put in an aquarium."

"I want it, Dad." Sapphire stood, still mesmerized by the fish's beauty.

"Are you sure?" her dad asked, looking at her.

"Yes, I'm sure... It's pretty." Sapphire touched the aquarium glass and the fish got startled and swam behind the castle in the aquarium.

"No touching of the glass!" One of the workers shouted from behind the counter.

"Sorry, she won't do it again," Sapphire's mother said, lightly pulling her daughter's hand from the aquarium. Sapphire was then left with her mom while her dad went to pick out an aquarium for the fish, but something else caught her eye. In a little box across the hall were six hamsters.

"What kind of rats are those, mom?" asked Sapphire, she was a little confused as they looked different from the rats the pet store worker was feeding the boa constrictor a little while ago.

"Those are not rats." Her mother chuckled, "They're hamsters."

Sapphire stood looking at the box with the hamsters. There were six in total and five of them all slept together in a corner. They looked pretty much the same with black and white fur, except for the smaller brown one that was alone on the other side of the box. Sapphire stood over the box looking at the hamsters; the brown one looked up at her and crawled across in her direction. Sapphire pointed at the brown one and said to her father who just returned with a small aquarium for the angel fish, "I want that one, daddy."

"Didn't you just say you wanted an Angel fish?" asked her father, placing the aquarium on a table.

"I want them both," Sapphire insisted.

"No, no, no, no, no… You will need to choose the hamster or the fish," said her mom, sternly looking at her.

"Aw man," said Sapphire as she bit her lip looking at the hamster and the Angelfish. *Hmm… this will be hard,* she thought to herself. Then she sang aloud, while pointing at angelfish and the brown hamster, "Inny Mini, Miney, Moe. One of the fish or the hamster will get to go."

Her finger then pointed at the small brown hamster. "Okay I will choose the hamster."

"Are you sure? This one looks so small," her dad said, looking at all the hamsters in the box.

"Yes, I want that one because it looks lonely, and I can make it happy."

"Okay if that's your choice." Sapphire's dad looked at her mom. "Let's get out of here quickly before she changes her mind again."

"I agree," her mom said, and they burst out laughing. Her father stretched his hand into the box to take out the brown one when the others awoke. They ran in front of the brown hamster, causing Sapphire's dad to pick up a black and white hamster instead and placed it in the blue cage that hung on the wall. Taking a bag of sawdust too, he walked towards the counter.

"What do hamsters eat daddy?"

"Well, pet hamsters eat pellets," he replied, holding up a bag of pellets to show her. Placing it on the counter with the sawdust and the hamster in the cage, he proceeded to pay the cashier. Sapphire was excited, she couldn't wait to reach home to play with her hamster.

She stood there looking at the cage and her hamster, but something was wrong, this was not the hamster she wanted.

"Dad… that's not the hamster I wanted!" Sapphire shouted, folding her arms.

"It's okay Sapphire," her father answered, "I thought I picked up the brown one, don't you want this one instead?"

"No! I want the brown one Daddy." Sapphire pointed towards the box with the other hamsters.

"Honey, just go back down the aisle and change the hamster before your daughter faints," her mother said smiling.

"Yeah," said Sapphire, still folding her arms and pouting her lips. So Sapphire and her father went back down the aisle with the cage to exchange the hamster. When they arrived at the box, as soon as Sapphire's dad opened the cage, the black and white hamster tried to escape.

"Oh no you don't!" shouted Sapphire's dad as he caught it midair, then placed it back in the box with the others. All the other hamsters were now rushing for his hand, climbing over the brown hamster in the process. However, this time, Sapphire's dad made sure he picked up the brown one. Sapphire was excited; she got her brown pet hamster.

"What are you going to call her?" asked her father, "Brownie?"

Sapphire thought for a little while and said, "I think I'm going to call her Hammy — Hammy the Hamster!"

"Okay, Hammy, welcome to our family." Her father laughed. They purchased the hamster, then left the pet store.

Chapter Two: Being Responsible

When Sapphire and her parents returned home, her dad placed the hamster cage on the table in the living room, then turned to Sapphire and asked, "Do you want the hamster to be happy?"

"Yes Daddy, and her name is Hammy."

"Okay." Her father laughed, "Do you want Hammy to be healthy?"

"Of course, Daddy."

"Then you need to be responsible, okay? You need to make sure Hammy is fed and has water to drink every day or else she will get hungry and thirsty and get very sick and will be sad."

"Yes Daddy, I will be responsible," Sapphire promised, then wondered, biting her lips, "Wait… what does it mean to be responsible, Daddy?"

"To be responsible is to do what you are supposed to do," her father responded. "So, you have a pet hamster named Hammy. To be responsible means you have to take care of her by making sure she is fed and has water to drink. You also need to make sure that her cage is clean every week so that it does not smell, okay?"

He then opened the cage and showed her how to put the sawdust in with the water and food.

"Why do I need to clean the cage, Daddy?" asked Sapphire.

Sapphire's dad chuckled to himself as he placed the bag of sawdust under the table. He then asked, "If you don't clean your room for a week, it will get dirty and smelly, correct?"

"Yes Daddy."

"Okay…how do you think you will feel if you start sleeping in a room that's smelly and dirty?" asked her father.

"I will not feel good, Daddy."

"Correct, so just as you need to be responsible to clean your room every week, you need to clean Hammy's cage. This is her room, and if it is not clean, she will be sad, okay?"

So Sapphire's dad made her promise that she would be responsible and feed Hammy and make sure her cage was cleaned every week.

Time passed for Sapphire and Hammy. She loved her pet so much. Hammy grew large and her fur was glossy. Every day Sapphire made sure to feed Hammy; she made sure Hammy had water to drink and cleaned her cage when it was dirty. Sapphire was responsible, and because she was responsible, Hammy was happy and because Hammy was happy, Sapphire was happy as well.

When Sapphire came home from school she would go to the cage and tell Hammy how her day was. She played with Hammy and loved to pet her. She even carried Hammy out to her backyard, so her pet could spend time out of the cage. She also loved watching Hammy run on the wheel; it was Hammy's favorite activity, and she did it every day. Sapphire and Hammy were no longer lonely because they had each other.

Chapter Three: The Break-In

It was soon to be Sapphire's birthday, just one more day, and she was excited. Her friends from school would be coming over and she could show them her pet hamster. She had told them all about Hammy and couldn't wait to show them her beloved pet.

She left with her parents to go to the city for balloons and other decorations for her birthday party. While at the store she saw a man making jewelry with colorful beads. They looked so pretty. Sapphire had a great idea–she will get matching bracelets for her and Hammy. Sapphire could wear hers on her wrist and Hammy around her neck. So she asked her dad and he bought both bracelets. They had different colors with the words 'I love you' affixed to them.

Sapphire was excited, she couldn't wait to reach home to give the bracelet to Hammy. However, when they returned, something horrible had happened. Their door was opened, and their house was ransacked— they were robbed.

"Oh my gosh! We were robbed!" Sapphire's dad exclaimed, then suggested, "Let's look around to see what was stolen." Sapphire immediately went to her room to look for Hammy but couldn't find her pet or the cage where she put it. She then went to all the rooms in the house. "Hammy!" she shouted but she could not find Hammy or the cage. Sapphire started to cry because she realized Hammy was stolen.

"Don't worry Sapphire," her father said as he hugged her, "I will get you a new hamster tomorrow, okay?"

"No, I don't want a new hamster!" Sapphire cried, "I want Hammy back." Sapphire hugged her mom and dad crying and whispered, "Please come back Hammy, please come back." Sapphire was distraught, this was the worst thing that could happen. She had nowhere to look, and Hammy was gone and there were no clues of where to look for her.

The police arrived shortly after. One dusted areas in the house for fingerprints, one took photos of the mess, and the last one was interviewing Sapphire's parents.

"There has been a lot of break-ins in the village recently," the officer said, "We will do our best to ensure these criminals are brought to justice."

Sapphire walked up to the police officer who was interviewing her mom and dad and said, "Mr. Policeman sir, can you please find Hammy?"

"Who's Hammy?" asked the policeman, turning to look at her.

"It's my Hamster and my best friend," she replied as she placed her arm around her dad. "She was stolen by the bad men who broke into our house."

"Oh, I'm so sorry Hammy was taken," said the policeman, making notes in his diary. "We will try our very best to get Hammy back to you and all the stuff that was taken from your house, okay?"

"Okay," Sapphire said, burying her face in her dad's stomach, weeping.

"It will be okay," Sapphire's dad assured her, gently rubbing her back.

Suddenly a voice came over the policeman's walkie-talkie. "There is a report of two men in a vehicle driving recklessly along the Eastern Main Road in Mt. Hope, in a blue Nissan Sentra coming from the Riverside area. Any officers in the area?"

The policeman who was conducting the interview took up his walkie-talkie and said, "Patrol 6530 presently in Riverside and will pursue."

He then turned to Sapphire and her parents and said, "We don't know if these are the guys, we will contact you if we receive any new information." They hurried to their vehicle and drove off.

Sapphire was hopeful that those were the bad guys, and they would be caught and Hammy would be safe in her arms again. "Be strong just for a little while again, Hammy," she muttered to herself.

Later that night Sapphire's dad was contacted by the police to come to the station urgently. The men that were described on the walkie-talkie earlier were captured, and they had stolen items with them. The police wanted Sapphire's mom and dad to identify if any of the stolen items were theirs. Sapphire, with her mom and dad, went to the station and were carried to a room where the stolen items were. The police informed them that the items were retrieved when they had captured the thieves in the forest.

"Can you identify any of these as yours?" one of the policemen asked Sapphire's parents. Sapphire's mom breathed a sigh of relief. Most of the items in the room were theirs.

Sapphire looked frantically around the room. Suddenly she saw, in the corner, Hammy's cage. "Hammy!" she shouted as she ran to the cage. She was so happy because she was about to get her hamster back, but to her surprise, the cage was broken and Hammy was not there.

"Where is Hammy?" she shouted as she looked at the officer. "Where is my Hamster?"

"I'm sorry," the policeman said. "When we captured these men, the cage was already broken... there were no hamsters in it."

"Oh no!" screamed Sapphire, "Hammy is alone in the forest by herself? You have to find her!" shouted Sapphire at the police officer.

"We brought everything we found at the scene," the police officer said calmly, "We did not see any hamster."

"You need to find her," cried Sapphire, "She's all alone." She then angrily stomped her feet on the ground and ran into her mom's arms crying. "She's all alone mummy. We have to find her."

"Please forgive my daughter, her hamster is very important to her and she is upset," her mother said to the policeman.

"I understand," the policemen replied, nodding.

"Where were they found?" Sapphire's dad asked the police officer. "We found them at the Arena Forest in Arima. The thieves just burnt their vehicle and were about to run into the forest when we captured them."

"Will we be able to go there tomorrow?" asked Sapphire's dad.

"Sure, you can," replied the police officer, "We already canvassed the area and our CSIs visited the scene."

Sapphire and her parents left the station. Sapphire was sad but hopeful that they would find Hammy the next day. When she reached home, she knelt by her bed and prayed that Hammy was safe and would be found.

The next day Sapphire was up early. She woke her dad and they both left for Arena Forest. When they arrived at the edge of the roadway, they saw the burnt remains of the car the robbers had set afire the day before. Sapphire started searching around the vehicle.

"Hammy! Hammy!" she shouted as they walked towards a small pathway. "Don't go too far," her father called, as he scanned the forest.

"We should still be careful; the robbers may not be here but we should still look out for dangerous animals."

Suddenly Sapphire saw something familiar in the pathway. It was the Hamster wheel from Hammy's cage by some rocks on the side of a tree. "Look Daddy!" shouted Sapphire, running towards the broken wheel. "There's Hammy's wheel!"

She then started shouting for Hammy. She and her dad looked around the area for a long time, when her father looked at his watch, saying, "It's been over an hour, Sapphire. Let's start on our way home; Hammy isn't here."

"Can we just look for five more minutes please Daddy? Hammy is here somewhere and needs us, I can feel it." So Sapphire and her dad searched along the path for another five minutes but Hammy could not be found.

Next to a tree close to the end of the path on their way back to their vehicle, Sapphire's dad saw a snake. It was a medium-sized snake coiled up facing a hole in the ground. "Wait Sapphire," said her dad as he held her hand. Sapphire was startled when she saw the snake and stepped a few paces back. She didn't like snakes ever since she saw the men at the pet store feeding them rats to eat.

Her dad then took up a stick and chased the snake into the hole. "It's not safe Sapphire, we've been here a long time, let's go back home."

Her dad was right, she was tired and sad, and it was time to go home. She hoped that the snake had not harmed Hammy and her pet hamster was still alive.

On the way back down the path, she went towards the broken hamster wheel by the rocks. She took out Hammy's bracelet she had brought and placed it on the wheel.

"Are you sure you want to leave it there?" asked her father.

"Yes, Daddy," she replied. "Hammy will see it and know I'm still looking for her." They then went back to the vehicle and returned home.

Part Two: Through the Eyes of Hammy

This part of the book explores the life of Hammy the Hamster through her eyes. Hammy had a tough life and thought it would never get better, then she received hope and a best friend. As we look through part two, Hammy carries us on an epic journey filled with lots of adventure. How will it end? Only one way to find out; sit back, relax, and let's read part two to see how this amazing adventure ends.

Chapter Four: Hammy's Life at the Pet Store

Before becoming Sapphire's pet, Hammy had been living in a box with eight other hamsters. These eight hamsters were a family. As time went by, three of the hamsters were bought, leaving behind the father, mother and their three remaining kids: Pip, Pippin, and Porky.

They didn't like Hammy. The mother and father hamsters told Hammy that they were the first hamsters that were brought in by the pet store owner, and their children must be selected first as pets before Hammy is selected. They took most of the food and Hammy had very little to drink; the other hamsters grew large and fluffy while Hammy was small and weak.

They climbed over her when someone was looking at the hamster box to ensure she wasn't selected. Each person who came into the pet store looking for a hamster always took the black and white ones instead of Hammy.

"You don't belong here," Pippin said one day, "Your owners didn't want you so they threw you away."

Hammy was too young to remember how she came to the pet shop. She had been just a baby, and she didn't remember her mother or father and didn't know if she had any brothers or sisters. It was rumored that someone found her on the side of the road as a baby, brought her to the pet store, and gave her to the owners. *Just once* she wished, *just once I would like someone to come and choose me.*

One day just like any other, the pet store workers came and left food for the hamsters, and as usual, the mother and father hamster with their kids Pip, Pippin, and Porky ate most of the food, barely leaving any for Hammy. The other hamsters were full and curled up in a corner and slept. Hammy ate the scraps that were left behind, but she still was very hungry and thirsty. Hammy felt so weak and could barely move.

Why won't they share the food and water with me? she thought to herself. "I'm so hungry and thirsty. I feel so weak," Hammy said as she started to cry. "I wish I get picked by someone, who will take care of me."

Suddenly she looked up and saw a little girl staring at her, smiling and pointing in her direction. Hammy got up; she was too hungry and weak to run so she started crawling towards the girl. She saw a man stretching his hand towards her. This was it, this was the moment she was waiting for—she was finally going to be chosen to be taken as a pet!

 Suddenly the other hamsters Pip, Pippin, and Porky got up and ran over her, causing the man to pick Pippin instead. "Goodbye Pippin, have a great life," said the mother hamster, smiling as the man took him out of the box.

The mother Hamster then turned towards Hammy and said, "Did you think it was going to be so easy? You would never leave this place until all of my kids go first."

Hammy started to cry and they all laughed at her, she thought she would have been chosen this time, she was sure the girl would have chosen her.

Suddenly Pip shouted, "Look, ma, the man is coming back; they want more hamsters!" They all ran over Hammy so the man wouldn't see her.

Suddenly they heard Pippin shouting, "I'm not going back, I'm getting out of here!" Then he dove out of the man's hands. However, the man was quick and caught him mid-air and placed him back into the box.

"He wants me instead," said Pip and he and his brother Porky started pushing each other towards the man.

"Come on boys," said the father hamster, "today is one of your lucky days."

However, the man continued pushing them aside heading for Hammy who looked up feebly and saw the same little girl looking at her, smiling. Hammy knew that this was it; she had finally gotten an owner. Her wish had at last come true. She would no longer be in the box with the wicked hamsters ever again.

The man picked her up and placed her in the cage. Hammy looked back at the other hamsters and started smiling. She was finally free. She waved her little paw at them and said a simple, "Goodbye!"

Chapter Five: Hammy's New Life

Hammy was carried to her new home, at #176 Riverside Avenue Mt. Hope. She had a big blue cage. This was the most room she'd ever had in her entire life. She had a wheel that she loved running on, and she loved going around and around the wheel. Running on the hamster wheel was her favorite thing to do. Her new owner, Sapphire, brought a toy bed so she could sleep in and a huge bowl for her food; she also had a water bottle to drink water when she was thirsty.

Hammy was so happy she did not live at the pet store anymore, with the wicked Hamsters who ate most of the food and drank most of the water. Her new owner, Sapphire, was responsible. Sapphire made sure she had plenty of food to eat and water to drink every day. Also, every week, Sapphire made sure she cleaned her cage, removing the old sawdust and replacing it with new sawdust. Sapphire also carried her into the backyard so she could run about and play in the grass. The air was so fresh, there were so many beautiful flowers, and she could hear birds chirping as she and Sapphire lay on their backs, watching the sky.

 Hammy loved playing in the backyard with Sapphire. *Sapphire is so responsible,* thought Hammy, *she makes sure I eat and drink and I have a clean place to live.* Hammy loved spending time with Sapphire. Every day they were together, Hammy would get a warm feeling in her heart. It felt so good! Hammy had never felt this way before. She would spend most of her day running on her wheel, but eagerly awaited when Sapphire would come home from school. Whenever Sapphire returned, she would tell Hammy all about her day. They were best friends. Hammy had so much to eat and drink, and because Sapphire took great care of her, Hammy grew large and her fur was fluffy.

Chapter Six: Ham-napped

One day when Sapphire and her parents left, Hammy went about exercising on her wheel when she heard a loud noise, like the sound of glass breaking. It was the glass window next to the TV in the living room. Hammy saw the glass was shattered, and two men dressed in black with masks covering their faces, climbed inside.

Hammy became afraid as they started going from room to room taking items and placing them into a big black bag. The house was in a mess.

Hammy ran behind her bed trembling, peeping at the burglars as they opened the front door and were about to leave when they stopped.

One of the men then turned and spotted Hammy. *Oh no!* Hammy thought as they approached her "Leave me alone... stranger danger! Stranger danger!" she squeaked, but there was no one to hear her. The man grabbed her cage and walked out of the house. Hammy was terrified, and she squealed as they took her and left the house.

As they were walking out to their vehicle, she turned around looking at the house that she and Sapphire lived in. It was a white house with a red mailbox and a red roof. The mailbox had the number 176 on it. The men then placed her into the trunk of the vehicle with all of the items they had stolen and drove away.

Hammy was lost, she could not see anything in the trunk of the car. It was dark and she had no idea where she was being taken or how to get back home. She knew when Sapphire came home, she would be very sad. Hammy too was sad because she knew deep down that she may never see her best friend Sapphire again.

Suddenly she felt the vehicle come to a stop and the trunk was opened. Squinting her eyes, she looked up and saw the men started unpacking the bags. They then took up the cage and proceeded to walk towards a path that led deep into what seemed to Hammy like a forest.

Hammy turned around just in time to see the other man lighting the vehicle on fire. Hammy was glad they didn't forget her in the trunk of the car. Suddenly, Hammy heard loud voices; it was police officers shouting at the robbers, they were surrounded.

The two men dropped the bags and the cage Hammy was in and placed their hands in the air. The cage fell on a rock and broke open.

Now's my chance, Hammy thought, and ran as fast as her little legs could carry her deep into the forest and away from the men. Hammy didn't look back, she kept running with all her might, deeper and deeper into the forest until she could run no more. She saw a heap of dry leaves and bushes between the roots of a tree and thought it would be a great place to rest and take a nap.

"I'm tired," Hammy said to herself as she settled between the roots under the dry leaves and fell asleep.

Chapter Seven: Lost

Hammy was deep in sleep when she was awoken by a loud noise. "HOOT...HOOT!!!" *What is that?* Hammy thought as she peeped from under the dry leaves but couldn't see anything except trees and bushes.

She looked up, the stars looked so bright and the moon was large, and then she heard it again. "HOOT...HOOT!!!"

"There it is again," Hammy said as she started scanning the bushes and trees again. There she saw, up on the branch of a tree right in front of her, was an owl. It was big and scary looking. Its feathers were brown, black, and gray and its head was moving from side to side searching the forest.

"I hope he doesn't see me," whispered Hammy, "That owl looks hungry and I don't want to be its next meal."

Hammy then heard a voice whispering in her ear. "SSSSSSS... I won't worry about you being the owl's next meal.... Because you are my next meal. SSSSS..."

She turned and it was a snake coiled up right behind her hissing and licking its lips. This snake was a boa constrictor like the one back at the pet store, but it was much larger! And it loved eating rats, squirrels, lizards, and possums.

Hammy knew this was bad news and screamed and tried to run out of the bushes but it was too late, the snake's tail quickly wrapped around her and started to squeeze. Hammy struggled as much as she could, but the snake was too strong.

"Let me go!" Hammy shouted as she struggled to escape. The dry leaves and bushes started scattering about as they both wrestled in the bushes.

"Why would I let you go?" hissed the snake, "I haven't eaten in 3 days—there is no way I'm going to let a nice plump hamster like yourself get away. I haven't eaten one of you in such a long time; you look tasty."

Hammy started screaming; the snake was now wrapped around her entire body, only her head was free. With all the ruckus, the dry leaves and bushes in which they were hiding were scattered all over the place. They were now in the open. The snake squeezed tighter and tighter. Hammy started to lose consciousness.

"Stop fighting," hissed the snake. "It's no use, you will be my dinner soon enough."

Suddenly they heard the owl. "HOOT.HOOT!!! What have we here?" said the owl as he swooped down from the branch and snatched the snake with its sharp talons and flew off. The snake, however, did not let go of Hammy, so the owl was flying through the sky holding the snake which was holding Hammy.

"Let me go!" screamed Hammy as the owl went higher and higher. The owl then tightened its claws into the snake, causing the snake to have no choice but to release Hammy so he could try and escape the owl. As a result, Hammy fell through the sky. "Ahhhhhhhh!!!!!" Hammy screamed as she hurled towards the ground and landed in a clump of leaves at the edge of the forest.

Hammy was out of breath and couldn't move. The snake had squeezed her so hard, she felt like all the air was squeezed out of her, making her too weak and tired to move.

"At least I'm alive. I thought I was a goner," Hammy said.

She then heard a voice behind her in a hole next to the bushes, "I thought you were goner too…it's not every day we see someone escape a snake and an owl at the same time."

"Ahhhh!" screamed Hammy. She was startled at the voice. She looked behind her and saw a hole in the ground with a heap of pebbles on either side. There was a mouse peeping from the hole.

"If you want to live you should come over to my burrow. There are lots of predators at night that hunt animals like you and me."

Hammy didn't move, she was afraid to go to the mouse.

"I don't know you," said Hammy, "I should not go with anyone I do not know, you are a stranger."

Suddenly Hammy heard the owl again. "HOOT…HOOT!!!" Hammy got so scared she ran past the mouse into the burrow.

"Well hello!" said the mouse. "I'm Sunny, I'm a wood mouse. What's your name?"

"I'm Hammy."

"Well now that we've exchanged names, we are not strangers. Are you hungry Hammy?" asked Sunny.

"Yes, I'm starving," replied Hammy.

"Okay, give me a sec," replied Sunny as she went deeper into the burrow. She came back with nuts and berries.

"I hope you like it. I got it earlier today," said Sunny.

"It's tasty," Hammy replied. She was used to pellets which she got from the pet store and her owner Sapphire. She had never eaten nuts or berries before.

"It's so good," Hammy said, and she ate until her belly was full. "I've never eaten nuts and berries before. Where do you get them?" asked Hammy.

"You're not from around here huh?" asked Sunny.

"No, I'm not," replied Hammy and she went on to tell Sunny where she lived at the pet store with other evil hamsters who ate all the food, giving her little to eat and drink and she was always hungry and thirsty.

And she also told Sunny about being chosen by Sapphire who took her home and took really good care of her. She then told her about the bad men who stole her and that she was now lost and didn't know how to get back home.

"Wow... I'm sorry to hear all that," Sunny said, "Sapphire sounds like a nice girl"

"She is!" replied Hammy, "She's the best!"

"Well, you are a lucky hamster after all that you went through. I heard screaming when I peeped out my burrow, and I saw you flying with a snake and an owl who would have both eaten you but you still got away... you must be tired."

"Yes, I am," replied Hammy.

"Well, get some rest." Sunny then carried her to a different part of the burrow; it had a bed made of bits of paper and leaves. "You can sleep here for the night, it's not what you are used to but I'm sure you'll get a good night's sleep."

Hammy went on the bed, it was comfy. She then looked at Sunny. "Thank you, Sunny."

"Don't mention it," replied Sunny, "Us smaller animals got to stick together."

Sunny then left. Hammy yawned and fell asleep.

Chapter Eight: New Friends

The next morning Sunny went to where Hammy was sleeping to wake her.

"Morning Hammy, time to get up," Sunny said as she came into the room.

"I'm so tired," Hammy replied as she yawned and stretched her arms and legs while looking at the ceiling. "Give me 5 more minutes."

"You can sleep later," answered Sunny, "I want you to meet my friend, he's outside waiting for you."

"Okay," Hammy said, and she and Sunny went outside. When they reached outside, on a root next to the burrow were some small rocks, and on top of the rocks was a squirrel eating nuts.

Sunny walked up to the squirrel and said, "Hello Chip, this is Hammy, my friend."

"Hello Hammy, pleased to meet ya! Glad to see you are still alive," greeted Chip, then he pointed at a tree down the path, "I live right by that tree down there near the opening."

Suddenly this path looked familiar to Hammy. A short distance away from Chip's tree was the burnt car that belonged to the robbers who had kidnapped Hammy the night before.

"Hold on," said Hammy, "I was there yesterday… with the fire… and ran away when I escaped the robbers."

"Yup, I saw you. It was a big commotion," Chip said, "I could've hardly breathed with all the smoke from the fire."

"The mistake you made is that you ran deep in the forest. We don't go deep in the forest, especially at night," Sunny said.

"That's right," Chip said, "That's where the predators live. You already met Slyther the snake and Oliver the owl. You are lucky to be alive."

"They were scary," Hammy said, "I hope I don't have to see them again."

"Yup, you are safer out here at the edge of the forest. Oliver and Slyther mostly stay deep in the forest. They only come to these parts if they can't get food then they come looking for us," said Sunny.

"That's why we don't ever come out at night… it's too dangerous," said Chip.

"So since you will be with us for a while, you gotta remember these things okay?" said Sunny.

"Okay, beware of Slyther the snake and Oliver the owl. I will remember that," said Hammy.

Although Hammy was happy she met new friends, she was still sad because she missed Sapphire and wanted to get back home. She missed playing on her wheel in her cage and hearing Sapphire talk about her day when she came back from school. Hammy didn't know how, but she believed one day she would see Sapphire again.

Suddenly there was a humming sound in the air, it was a hummingbird flying towards them.

"Hello guys, who's your friend?" said the hummingbird.

"Jubilee!" shouted Sunny and Chip.

"Hey guys, long time no see," said Jubilee.

"Hello I'm Hammy the Hamster."

"Hello Hammy," said Jubilee, "What brings you to our neck of the woods?"

Hammy went on to tell her story, how she lived in the pet store and was taken by Sapphire to live with her. She went on to tell her story about being stolen by the robbers and escaping into the forest and almost being eaten by Slyther and Oliver.

Suddenly she heard a familiar sound down the path; the sound of a little girl. "Hammy!...Hammy!"

Hammy could not believe it, it was Sapphire walking up the path towards them.

"There she is!" shouted Hammy, "That's my person... Let's go meet her guys."

Hammy was excited. She was so happy, she couldn't believe it; right down the path was Sapphire and her dad walking towards them.

"Awesome," said Jubilee, "You'll be home soon."

Chapter Nine: Slyther and His Brothers

Hammy and her friends were about to go down the path to Sapphire when suddenly there was a rustling in the bushes and a voice emerged, "You all are not going anywhere!" It was Slyther the snake and he was with his two brothers, Fangs and Scales.

They crawled out of the bushes and surrounded Hammy, Sunny, and Chip. Jubilee got scared and flew away. Slyther was covered with scratches all over his body and his eye. Licking his lips, he hissed, "Oh, there is my dinner from last night, brothers."

Slyther then turned to Hammy. "I need to pay you back, hamster. Because you were struggling with me last night, Oliver the owl picked me up and was carrying me to his nest so I had to drop you. I fought for my life, Oliver scratched me all over my body and I lost an eye. Now I only have one good eye," hissed Slyther.

"It's time for revenge brother," hissed Fangs.

"Yesss," hissed Scales, "Looks, there is a meal for each of us— one hamster, one squirrel, and one wood mouse… I'm sure you all are tasty".

Sunny then looked around, they were surrounded, and there was nowhere to go; nowhere but back to her burrow.

"Run guys!" Sunny shouted, "Let us go to my burrow!"

They all rushed inside Sunny's burrow.

Slyther turned to his brothers and said, "Scales, you stand watch outside the burrow. Fangs and I will follow them."

"Okay brother," replied Scales.

Slyther and Fangs then followed Hammy and the others into the burrow.

Inside the burrow, there was an intersection with two different paths. "Which way to go?" Hammy asked Sunny.

"We need to split up," replied Sunny.

"I don't like this idea," said Chip, "We should stick together."

"Don't worry I have a plan," answered Sunny, "The burrow is long and has two different holes. Slyther and his brothers will follow us, but I know this burrow like the back of my paw, it's my home. There is a way out so listen carefully, okay?"

"Okay," Hammy and Chip agreed, nodding.

"Hammy and Chip, you take the hole to the left and I'll go to the right. Go straight to the back of the burrow, there will be another hole that will lead you outside, but do not go through as yet, wait until you see the snake, okay?"

Hammy and Chip nodded, "Okay."

Sunny continued, "Do you remember the small rocks outside the entrance of my burrow?"

"Yes," said Chip. "Okay, here's what I want you to do, when you see the snakes, crawl out of the hole and push the small rocks to cover the hole, that way the snake will not be able to come out. I will do the same to close the hole on my end of the tunnel, then, I will run around to the entrance and push the rocks to cover that hole. Deal?"

"Deal," replied Hammy and Chip as they went to the hole on the left and Sunny to the right.

Meanwhile, Slyther and Fangs entered the burrow.

"I'll take the left and you take the right," said Slyther to Fangs.

"Okay," replied Fangs as they split up and went down the different holes in the burrow.

Meanwhile, at the back of the burrow, Sunny, Chip, and Hammy waited patiently for the snakes. Sunny was poised, looking nervously down the burrow, when she saw Fangs approaching, closer and closer. As soon as Fangs reached close enough, Sunny darted out of the hole and quickly pushed the rocks blocking the hole.

"Hey!!!" shouted Fangs, "What's the big idea?"

"Hope you like your new home because you will be there for a while!" shouted Sunny as she ran around to the entrance of her burrow, but to her surprise, Scales the snake was still there.

Oh no, thought Sunny, *If I'm unable to close the hole at the entrance of my burrow, the snakes will escape.* So Sunny stood hidden behind a tree, looking at Scales when she saw a man and a little girl. It was Hammy's person, Sapphire and her dad. He picked up a stick and chased Scales away. Scales was so afraid, he crawled into the burrow and didn't come out.

Sunny stayed behind the tree as Sapphire and her dad left. As soon as they disappeared down the path, she quickly ran to the burrow's entrance and pushed the rocks to block the hole, trapping Scales inside

Now it's just for Hammy and Chip to escape and block the other hole with the rocks and the snakes will be trapped, thought Sunny. Meanwhile Hammy and Chip were waiting on their side of the burrow for the snakes to show up so they could escape.

A loud hissing sound was heard and kept getting closer and closer.

"SSSSSSSS.... Hamster...Hamster...I know you are here with your friend. I can smell you through these walls and you smell good," hissed Slyther.

"I'm scared," whispered Hammy to Chip, "Let's get out of here."

"No, we can't just yet," replied Chip, "Remember we have to stick to the plan. We have to wait until we see the snakes, then we go through the hole and block it with the stones."

"Okay," answered Hammy. So they both stood at the edge of the burrow waiting for the snakes when they heard Scales' and Fang's voices echoing throughout the burrow.

"Brother...Brother, it's a trap!" shouted Scales, "they are trapping us in the burrow. Don't let them get out or else they will push stones to block us in." Then there was silence.

Suddenly Slyther shot out from the corner towards them, crawling as fast as he could to try and make it before Hammy and Chip climbed out of the burrow.

"You will not escape me," he hissed as she slithered towards them. But it was too late. Hammy and Chip climbed out the hole of the burrow and pushed the rocks blocking it, trapping Slyther and his two brothers inside.

They ran over to where Sunny was at the main entrance of the burrow. They started jumping and laughing and singing "Snaky trapped in a hole. Snaky trapped in a hole. No more run. Let's have some fun. Snaky trapped in a hole!!!"

They then danced and pranced, laughing and singing. Suddenly Hammy remembered Sapphire was there a little while ago with her dad, and she ran down the path looking for them. She ran past the robbers' burnt car, but it was too late. They had already left.

Hammy started to cry. She was so close. Sapphire and her dad were so close. However, Slyther the snake and his brothers caused her to miss them. Then something caught her eye in the corner near the robbers' burnt car, on top of her hamster wheel, was a bracelet.

This was not there when I was in the cage, she thought, *this has to be from Sapphire.* She placed the bracelet around her neck.

At the same time, Sunny and Chip came down the path towards her. "I'm sorry you missed them," Sunny said, "Sapphire's dad helped us. He chased Slyther's brother Scales into my burrow, so I was able to trap him with the others."

"I'm sorry you lost your home as well Sunny," Hammy said.

"They won't be trapped there for long," said Sunny, "If they work together, they will be able to push through the rocks."

"Okay we would not want to be close when they get out," Chip said.

"Well it's not safe here anymore," Sunny said. "Slyther and his brothers will not go back to the deep forest until they catch us. So, it's time to look for a new home."

"I agree," replied Chip, "It's no longer safe here. Let's go to my tree. I have some nuts and I'm sure you guys are hungry."

"Yes," Hammy said, "I am hungry."

So they all left to go to Chip's tree to eat.

Chapter Ten: Homeward Bound

Hammy, Chip, and Sunny all sat next to the tree eating nuts, thinking about where they would go to live next.

"We need to find a new home, but we cannot go deep into the forest because the snake brothers will be looking for us, and Oliver the Owl lives there as well. They both want to eat us," said Sunny.

At that moment, there was a humming sound. "Did someone say new home?"

"Jubilee!" they all shouted as she landed next to them.

"Glad you guys are all safe," she replied. "It's only for a while," Sunny said, "those rocks can only hold them for a little while so we should start looking for a new place to live."

"Well, I have some news for you guys," said Jubilee. "Hammy, when we saw your person, Sapphire with her dad, those pesky snakes showed up and spoiled everything. We had to run for our lives, so I flew away, but guess what? I did not just fly away from the snake brothers, I followed your person. I know where they live."

"Really?!" Hammy said excitedly. She could not believe it. She just thought she lost Sapphire forever and now Jubilee brought this news.

"Hooray!" shouted Chip and Sammy. "Well," Jubilee said, "What are you guys waiting for? It's a bit of a long journey but if we leave now we will be there in no time."

"Okay," Hammy said, "Lead the way."

So, Jubilee flew off and Hammy followed. A short distance away, Hammy stopped and looked back at Chip and Sunny. "Aren't you guys coming?" Hammy said, "You guys do need a new home, right?"

"Are you sure we can come?" Sunny asked.

"Yeah," said Chip, "The humans we know about are not safe to be around. They don't like us being around them, so they chase us away."

"Don't worry my person, Sapphire is the best—est girl in the world. She and her parents will love us. Plus, I'm sure it will make Sapphire happy," Hammy said.

"Okay I'm in," said Chip.

"Me too," replied Sunny.

"Yay!!" Hammy replied. "This is so exciting, not only will I see Sapphire again, I will have even more friends to live with. Come with me."

So Hammy, Sunny, and Chip all followed Jubilee to where Sapphire lived.

"Okay as we are leaving the forest, remember we need to watch out for people and cars, so stay off the street. We don't want a car crushing us, okay? Also, only go when I say it's safe to do so."

They all agreed as they scurried across the street and onto the sidewalk. They walked for over an hour, listening to Jubilee when she said stop and when she said go. The view was pretty; they saw houses and cars in all different colors and sizes. Hammy started to think of sleeping in her bed again in her nice blue cage, but this time with her new friends Sunny and Chip.

"We are almost there," shouted Jubilee, "It's right up this street."

Hammy was so happy she was stolen, lost, almost eaten and now she was almost back home. She couldn't wait to see Sapphire again!

Suddenly they heard a purring sound, then a voice. "Well, Well, Well… this is not something you see every day, Tommy!" It was three cats on a wall looking down at them, licking their lips; Harry, Marv and Tommy.

"A pweety bird and some tasty tweets Harry," said Marv, and they started to laugh.

"Run guys!" Jubilee shouted to her friends. "The house is right there, it's the white house with the red mailbox."

Hammy looked up and could see it. Right across the street was the white house, with the red mailbox and the number 176 on it. To her surprise, Sapphire was in the gallery with her parents. Sapphire was looking on the ground.

There were a lot of cars driving down the street. It was too dangerous to cross but they had no choice, the cats were running after them, and they would catch them soon. Hammy, Chip, and Sammy ran across the street; Hammy was the slowest of them all. Before you know it, Sunny and Chip crossed the street and ran into Sapphire's yard. However, Hammy was only able to reach the middle of the road.

Hammy turned around and saw the cats. Marv was already over her with the other two, Tommy and Harry, close behind. They all smiled with open claws. "It's over you hamster...you are all mine!" shouted Marv as he stretched his paw to grab Hammy.

Tommy and Harry, a few feet behind Marv, were getting closer. It was all over, Hammy was so close but yet so far. There was nothing else Hammy could do. She was so afraid she could no longer move; she just closed her eyes and accepted her fate.

Then there was a loud screeching sound, followed by a 'thud'. Hammy opened her eyes and she saw Marv, smashing into a trash can across the street, rolling onto some garbage that was on the sidewalk.

A car that was driving down the street, had screeched to a halt, hitting Marv, sending him flying. Hammy was right next to the wheel; if the car had moved a few inches again, she would have been flattened. Marv got up from the garbage heap, purring in pain, "Me— ow! Me— ow! it hurts!"

He looked back at Hammy and limped off. The other two cats, Tommy and Harry, looked scared after seeing Marv get hit by the vehicle. They both looked at each other and ran off, following Marv, leaving Hammy trembling next to the car wheel. Then Hammy heard the sound of Sapphire's voice. "Hammy!!! Mommy, Daddy! It's Hammy, she came back to us... look."

Sapphire's dad came out into the street, picked up Hammy and brought her into the yard.

"How do you know it's Hammy dear?" asked Sapphire's mom.

"It is her," replied Sapphire, "Look, she has on the bracelet daddy, and I left in the forest."

"This is amazing," said her dad, "How can such a tiny hamster make her way home by herself from the forest which is so far away?" wondered Sapphire's dad.

"It's truly amazing," said her mom. "It's because Hammy is amazing and special." Sapphire giggled. Hammy was in Sapphire's arms again. It was so good; she always knew this day would happen again and it was finally here.

She turned to Chip and Sunny who were behind the plants and signaled for them to come out of hiding. Jubilee flew down, landing first on the mailbox, then down to the ground next to Sapphire. Sunny and Chip came out from behind the plants, next to Sapphire as well.

"Oh... are these your friends Hammy?" asked Sapphire as Hammy jumped down from her hands and went to her friends.

"It seems they are," her dad said. "That's probably why Hammy was able to make it back from the forest. She made friends and they helped each other along the way."

"It looks so," said Sapphire. Then she picked them all up, Sunny, Chip, and Hammy. Jubilee flew and landed on her shoulder. Sapphire then looked at her parents, giggling.

"Mommy, Daddy, can I keep them?" asked Sapphire, smiling at them.

Sapphire's dad looked at her mom and her mom looked at him and nodded.

"Only if you promise to be responsible and look after them properly," her dad said.

 "Yayyy!!!" Sapphire shouted, "I promise I will take care of you all, feed you, make sure you have enough to drink, play with you, and have so much fun. You too, birdy," Sapphire said as Jubilee started prancing on Sapphire's shoulder. They all went inside.

As promised, Sapphire took care of Hammy, Chip, and Sunny. Chip lived in an almond tree in Sapphire's backyard, and Sunny made a new burrow under that same tree. This made them so happy because they had all the nuts they could eat. There was also a small stream that passed through the backyard, so they had enough to drink as well. This made Chip and Sunny very happy because they were safe and had plenty to eat and drink.

Hammy's cage was no longer locked, she was free to go out into the backyard whenever she liked to play with and visit Chip and Sunny. Jubilee came and visited from time to time, telling them stories of the forest. Slyther and his brothers made it out of the burrow and were looking for Hammy and the others but had no idea where they were. Hammy and the others laughed so much because they knew that Slyther and his brothers would never find them.

Sapphire took very good care of them all. She sometimes brought friends over to play with all her pets. They were all very happy and had so much fun together. Sapphire, Hammy, Sunny, and Chip all became best friends and lived happily ever after.

Epilogue

The adventure for Sapphire has just ended. However, it has just begun for Hammy and her new friends. The world is such a big and amazing place. What new adventure awaits? Will Slyther and his brothers find Hammy and her friends? Will there be new dangers at their new home? Stay tuned for more epic adventures with Hammy and her new friends Chip, Sunny, and Jubilee as they explore this new world.

Coming Up Next in this epic series— Book 2: Jubilee and the Lost Eggs. Stay tuned!

About The Author

Jamal never envisioned himself as a writer. Growing up in the quaint village of Chinapoo, surrounded by the vibrant culture of his twin isles home of Trinidad and Tobago, his deep passion for sports developed at a young age.

Football (soccer), cricket, basketball, and even chess, became integral parts of his upbringing, shaping his character and instilling within him a wholesome competitive spirit. However, despite his dedication to sports, fate had other plans for him, when he stumbled upon a love for writing.

Encouraged by the unwavering support of his family and friends and driven by his innate creativity, he embarked on a transforming journey to explore this newfound passion; setting forth on a mission to become a versatile writer.

With each word penned, Jamal not only honors his love for writing but also pays homage to the rich tapestry of experiences that shaped his identity. It is his hope, through his diverse literary works, Jamal will inspire, entertain, and leave an indelible mark on the world.

And so, from the small village of Chinapoo to the vast realms of imagination, Jamal's journey as a writer continues to unfold, fueled by passion, perseverance, and the unwavering belief in the power of storytelling.

www.ingramcontent.com/pod-product-compliance
Lightning Source LLC
Chambersburg PA
CBHW060505160726

47992CB00003B/1333